Nimrod The Great

Written By:

Carol Kelly

Illustrations By:

Esther Gustaffsson-DeCook

WestBow Press books may be ordered through booksellers or by contacting:

WestBow Press
A Division of Thomas Nelson & Zondervan
1663 Liberty Drive
Bloomington, IN 47403
www.westbowpress.com
1 (866) 928-1240

ISBN: 978-1-4908-4800-6 (sc)
ISBN: 978-1-4908-4801-3 (e)

Library of Congress Control Number: 2014914692

Print information available on the last page.

WestBow Press rev. date: 3/27/2015

WESTBOW
PRESS
A DIVISION OF THOMAS NELSON
& ZONDERVAN

There once was a little boy called Nimmy, who was the son of a very wise and loving father. Nimmy adored his father and longed for the day that he would be just like him.

Nimmy watched everything his father did. Every day his father would rise early and spend much time within his study. Nimmy would sneak downstairs in his pyjamas most mornings hoping to discover what exactly his father did behind the large wooden study door. He would sit on the floor trying to imagine what his father was doing. "Hmmm, maybe he is counting all his money," thought Nimmy. "That's it!" whispered Nimmy. "After all, my father is a very wise man and he owns lots of cattle and sheep."

One morning, Nimmy sneaked downstairs in his pyjamas, and stood outside the door. He tried to peek through the keyhole but it was no good. He even tried to listen but all he could hear was a faint, distant mumbling. "Hmmm," sighed Nimmy as he sat on the floor and leaned against the door.

As he leaned there, he grew tired. His father seemed to stay in his study for the longest time ever. Eventually Nimmy's little eyes grew heavy and he fell asleep against the study door.

Nimmy awoke to the creaking of the study door and the laughter of his father. "Nimmy, son, what are you doing sleeping outside my study door?" his father asked. "Emm, nothing, Dad," Nimmy answered. "I just, emm ... well, I came down this morning to ask you something ... something important," stuttered Nimmy, "and I waited and waited and I must have fallen asleep."

Nimmy's Dad smiled. "What was it you wanted to ask me, Nimmy?" Nimmy paused and thought carefully. He was too shy to tell his father the real reason he came downstairs so he said, "I know Mr Brown is coming to paint the hay barn tomorrow, and I wanted to know if I could help him."

"Oh, I don't know if you are big enough yet to help with such a big job," replied Nimmy's Dad. "Maybe next time, son." Nimmy sighed. He wanted to help. He wanted to be useful. He wanted to be just like his father.

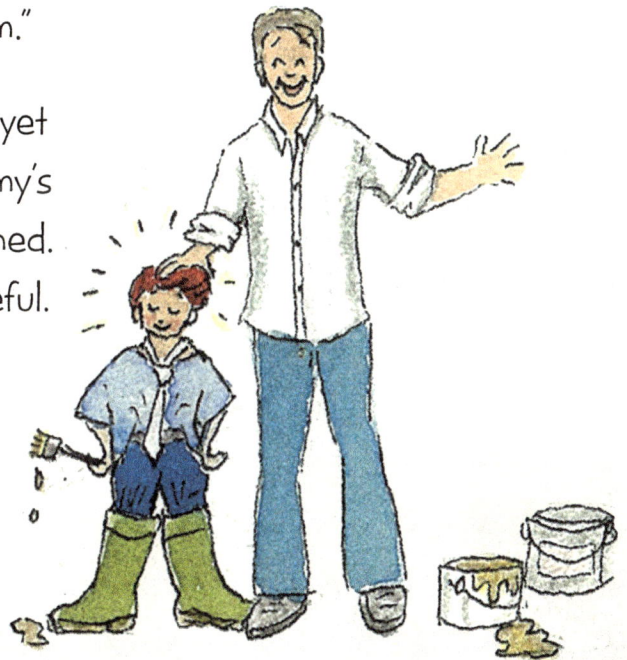

"Nimmy, I have to go to town today to pick up something very special," called Nimmy's Dad. "What are you getting?" asked Nimmy. "I can't tell you yet, son, but you will see when I return home." "Ok, Dad," said Nimmy. "Now, while I am gone you're in charge. Man the stations!" commanded Nimmy's Dad.

"Yes Sir!" saluted Nimmy, "you can count on me". "Ok soldier, to your post ... But you might want to change out of your pyjamas," said Nimmy's Dad as he got into his car. "Goodbye, Nimmy, I'll see you this afternoon," and his father drove up the dusty lane. "Bye, Dad, see you later," called Nimmy after him.

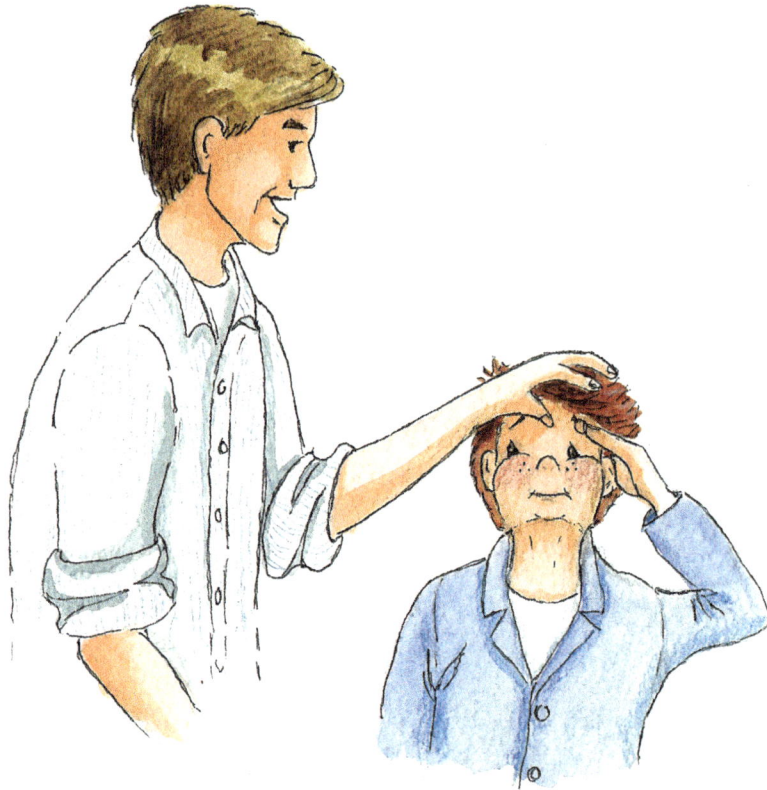

Nimmy watched his father's car as it disappeared in a cloud of dust down their driveway.

"Ok," he said, "I'm in charge. Let's get to work, soldier," and he smiled to himself.

Nimmy raced upstairs to change out of his pyjamas. As he looked in his wardrobe and pulled many clothes from his drawers, he realised that he had nothing manly to wear. "These are all little boy's clothes, I'm not a little boy anymore, I am Nimmy ... No, wait! I am Nimrod, yeah, Nimrod The Great!! I will prove to Dad that I am all grown up and that I am as wise as he is!"

At that Nimmy ran to his father's room and pulled out some of his father's clothes. "Yes!" exclaimed Nimmy, "this is much better".

He pulled on a shirt, trousers and even managed to tie one of his father's ties around his neck. "Ok, perfect," thought Nimmy. "No, wait, something is missing. Shoes!" He looked all around the room, but all he could see were his father's black, shiny, Sunday shoes.

"Hmm, not very good for walking around the farm in," thought Nimmy. "Oh, I know!" he whispered, clicking his fingers. "Dad's boots are at the back door!" Nimmy stood and admired himself in the mirror.

"Dad will be proud of me," he thought and with that he took off downstairs to find his father's boots, tripping over the very long ends of his father's trousers as he went.

Nimmy searched and found his father's boots at the back door. Pulling them on, he tried to stand up. "This is more difficult than I thought." He tried a second time with no success. The third time he reached for the window sill and pulled himself up. "Perfect," said Nimmy. "Hi, ho! Hi, ho! It's to my father's work I go," sang Nimmy, but with his first steps he tripped over his trouser leg. "Ouch! That hurt!" Nimmy sat on the ground and tucked the trouser legs into his father's large boots. "No more accidents," he thought as he pulled himself up again.

Off Nimmy plodded towards the hen-house to collect the eggs from the hens. "Oh boy, I bet the hens will think it is Dad coming when they see me." Nimmy had never really liked being close to the hens, and he had never even been inside the hen-house before, but today he wanted to prove to his father that he could do just as his father does.

Nimmy entered the hen-house and lifted a basket in his hand to collect the freshly laid eggs. "The hens must be all asleep," he thought. "That's great, I can take the eggs and go quickly." Nimmy took one of the eggs from the tray and placed it in his basket, nice and slowly. "See, this isn't too difficult," he said to himself. One by one he took the eggs until he had six.

There was just one egg left to pick up. As he reached in, he heard the hen cluck and flap its wings. At that all the other hens were startled and Nimmy jumped, throwing the basket in the air! Nimmy turned to escape out of the hen-house just as the eggs fell down upon his head! "Ouch! No!" said Nimmy as he clumsily stumbled out of the hen-house.

When he got outside, he realised he still had the basket in his hand, only it was empty and there was eggy goo running down from his hair. "Oh no, the eggs!" said Nimmy as he wiped the goo with the sleeve of his Dad's shirt. "Ok, so that didn't go so good and I will have to explain to Dad why we have no eggs for supper ... what will I do now? How can I prove that I am all grown up if I can't even gather eggs without leaving a mess?"

Nimmy looked down at his boots and the empty basket in his hand and thought. "Wait a minute, I am Nimrod! I am not going to be beaten by a few smashed eggs! I just need to find something bigger and better than this task ... Yeah, something that will make Dad proud of me. I know!" he exclaimed, "I will paint the barn. I know Dad said I am too small but if I paint it, it will show him just how grown up I am. Then he will see how wise I am and he won't have to pay Mr Brown to paint it tomorrow."

Nimmy set off for the barn singing, "Hi, ho! Hi, ho! It's to my father's work I go, I'll paint that old barn with my own bare arms, I will prove I'm wise before my father's eyes, for I am Nimrod the Great!!!"

Nimmy arrived at the barn to find tins of paint everywhere. "I wonder ... what colour did Dad want the barn to be painted?" thought Nimmy as he grabbed a paintbrush from the ground and looked at all the tins of paint. "Maybe I should try a few colours out. I want to make a wise choice."

Nimmy took the paint buckets outside and tried each colour one by one, yet he was still unable to decide. "Boy, this is hard work," said Nimmy, "but I am determined to make a wise choice." So he continued to try colour after colour.

"Maybe," he said, trying the blue. "I'm not sure," he thought, trying the green. "I can't decide," he sighed after trying red, yellow and orange.

"I need a rest." Nimmy sat down and leaned against the big oak tree beside the barn. He looked at all the colours he had painted on the barn. "I need wisdom," he said with a yawn. "I need wisdom like Dad has to make a good choice. Where can I find it though? I just don't know." And as he thought about it, he drifted off to sleep under the shade of the tree.

Nimmy awoke to the gentle nudging of his father. "Nimmy, Nimmy ... what happened to the barn? And my clothes ... and your hair?" Dad asked. "Oh, Dad, you're home," replied Nimmy. "Yes I am". "Dad, I've been so busy," said Nimmy. "As I can see, Nimmy. What has been going on?" asked his Dad.

"Dad, don't call me Nimmy anymore. I am Nimrod The Great. I am not a little boy anymore. Look! I decided to show you by painting the barn." "Oh right, Nimmy - sorry Nimrod," said Dad. "So why is the barn covered in so many colours?"

"Well," began Nimmy, "I guess I hoped that if I showed you how grown up I am that you would let me join you in your work in the study every morning. I just don't understand, Dad, you always get it right. I try but I mess up trying to prove that I am bigger and stronger and wiser than I am. I'm sorry, Dad, for making such a mess." "It's ok, son, we all make mistakes, and I have made many. I am only wise because the One I follow is wise," said Nimmy's Dad, smiling softly at his son. "The One you follow?" asked Nimmy.

"Yes, son, Jesus. Just like you, every morning I need to pray and ask for His help for every part of my day," replied Dad. "Every morning? Is that what you do in your study every morning, Dad?" exclaimed Nimmy. "Yes son." "Oh, I thought you were doing some great big work," Nimmy said. "I am, son, the time I spend with Jesus every morning is the most important work I do," answered Dad.

"Dad, so is Jesus wiser than you?" asked Nimmy. "Yes, son, He is the Son of God, He knows everything." "Everything? So I guess He knows I'm afraid of hens, and how silly I am when I try to do things on my own?" "Yes, He knows and He wants to help you. Jesus is our Good Shepherd and He knows how to lead us the best. We are like sheep, we get lost and get stuck in all sorts of trouble. Jesus wants us to call for His help and to ask for it every day."

"Dad, I just wanted to be like you," sighed Nimmy. "I know, son, and I want to be more like Jesus. Son, I am only a man, but Jesus is the Son of God our Saviour and He holds all wisdom," said Dad. "Wow, Dad, if He is wiser than you, I can't wait to talk with Him. I think me and Jesus are going to be great friends!" said Nimmy. "I hope so, son," smiled Dad.

"Now, Nimmy, what are we going to do about the barn?" Nimmy looked over at the barn and realised his choices didn't seem so wise after all. "I don't know, Dad, but I do know it is exhausting work trying to walk in your shoes when my feet are so little." "I'm sure it is, Nimmy," laughed Dad, "but in time you will grow into them. Just don't be too quick to grow up." "Ok, Dad," smiled Nimmy. "Maybe when I get older, I will make wise choices like you." "You will, Nimmy," replied Dad. "But do you know what is the wisest choice any boy or girl could ever make?" "What is it, Dad?" asked Nimmy.

"To follow Jesus every day of their life, Nimmy. That's the wisest choice of all." "Dad," said Nimmy quietly, "I don't know a lot about Jesus. How am I going to follow Him? Where do I start?"

"Good question, Nimmy," answered Dad. "The best place to start is by reading the Bible and that was why I had to make a special trip to town today. Here, son, when I was in town I got you your very own Bible to read."

"Oh, thank you, Dad!" said Nimmy. "This is so cool. Now I can learn all about Jesus for myself!" "Nimmy, now that you're growing up and have your own Bible, how would you like to join me in my study every morning and we could read and pray together?" "Really, Dad?" asked Nimmy, full of excitement. "Wow, Dad, I can't wait!"

"Great!" said Dad. "Now, you must be hungry after all that work, how about we go and make some scrambled eggs for lunch?"

"Em Dad ..." began Nimmy, "about the eggs ... "

The End

Acknowledgements

Author- Carol Kelly

Illustrated By- Esther Gustaffsson-DeCook

Co-Edited By – Shirley McHale & Bronagh Hayes